AREN MABLE

CREATIVITY RULES

**The Ultimate Guide on Creative Thinking,
Learn The Best Ways on How to Come Up
With Creative and Original Ideas**

Descrierea CIP a Bibliotecii Naţionale a României
AREN MABLE
   CREATIVITY RULES. The Ultimate Guide on Creative Thinking, Learn The Best Ways on How to Come Up With Creative and Original Ideas / Aren Mable – Bucharest: Editura My Ebook, 2021
   ISBN

AREN MABLE

CREATIVITY RULES

The Ultimate Guide on Creative Thinking, Learn The Best Ways on How to Come Up With Creative and Original Ideas

My Ebook Publishing House
Bucharest, 2021

TABLE OF CONTENTS

FOREWORD

"Whenever I think of something but can't think of what it was I was thinking of, I can't stop thinking until I think I'm thinking of it again. I think I think too much." – Criss Jami

Have you thought about something and been able to link it to other things without even realizing it? You were in the process of using your creative thinking. Everyone has their individually unique creativity. However, it is important that a person knows how to use and trigger it first before he/she will get the benefits of thinking creatively. Not all people get the chance to show off their creativity when thinking, so only some are able to become successful in their own chosen career.

There are some people who naturally have skills, while others need to practice and learn about them first before they can take advantage of them. Being able to think creatively is very important, especially if you want to become successful in your career or in your whole life. However, only some people realize this fact. So, if you are one of those people who are finding it hard to boost up their creative thinking skills, this book is primarily created for you.

This book contains some useful and helpful information about creative thinking and what you can do to obtain it.

Chapter 1

Creative Thinking Basics

Creativity can be triggered by specific things, especially when the person involved has the natural ability to do so. For a person with natural creative thinking skills, it naturally occurs even if he or she is not aware of it. Learn more about the basics of creative thinking in this chapter.

Creative Thinking and Its Fundamentals

What exactly is creativity? Indeed, there are a number of ways you can define the word "creativity". However, the most modest way to define this mysterious element that is shared by all people is the fact that creativity is the ability of the person's mind to acquire facts, materials, and/or ideas and distinguish them in a distinctive manner or way. It is a unique point of view, a fresh idea and/or a new way of looking at a certain problem.

A lot of people will tell you that they are not creative, or you may even think that you are not. But then, you have to realize that everyone is truly creative. Every person has his/her own creative style. A few are good at producing new ideas and playing around with them, making those ideas more functional, while others are simply fine when it comes to identifying unusually new solutions and ways of doing things.

Take a glance at your surroundings, at the house or apartment you are living in, at the fixtures and furniture in this space. Look at the clothes that you wear. Each manufactured product you view was, at one time or another, an idea or thought in a person's mind.

Each time you make a decision about something it is because your mind perceives the situation a certain way. Each time you make a decision on what to eat and what to wear, or how to organize something and get to work, you are being creative. When people envision a beautifully colored flower and then mentally change a few of its characteristics (such as its shape, texture, petal shape and more), no one will have the same image after five minutes. This is mainly due to the fact that everyone will produce a unique image. It only means that everyone is creative.

Creative thinking is a natural way of thinking and not a different way of thinking. You have been taught about thinking logically, reproductively and even linearly. Along with this, you might have been informed that creativity in itself should be learned and taught in the same manner as other subjects in academics. It should not be the case. Conceptual blending is in the center of imagination. It is a cognitive process, which functions under the consciousness level. This involves the association of 2 cognitive ideas to produce new meanings, while explaining creativity and abstract thoughts – an underlying mental process that is distinctive to humans. Constantly occurring without your awareness, these blends are vital for the conception of emergent ideas, global insight, and meanings.

With these ideas in mind, you should have a better understanding about the basics of creative thinking.

Chapter 2

Define Your Intent

"Others have seen what is and asked why. I have seen what could be and asked why not. " – Picasso

All things you do in life definitely have their individual purposes. But then, not every person realizes the importance of defining the intent prior to carrying on with things. This applies in the same way when using your creative thinking. Learn how to define your intent to boost your creative thinking in this chapter.

Know Your Purpose

Your purpose is what motivates you to go on with your journey in life. It is something that fuels you to do things and create more useful thoughts. This is where your creative thinking is triggered. By knowing your purpose, it should be much easier for you to use your creative thinking skills, allowing you to achieve your goals in the most creative way possible.

What exactly is your purpose and how will you find it if you don't know what it is? No matter what motivates you to jump out of bed each morning, regardless of what makes you excited, or no matter what your true passion is, it probably has something to do with your purpose.

As a person, you have your own distinctive format through which you like to live your purpose. To define your purpose is something that you can do through exploring and experiencing, allowing you to rediscover the real meaning of life. During the process of defining your purpose, you can apply your creativity and creative thinking into it. Since you yourself is the only one who can define your own purpose, you have the free will to choose how you want it to be.

Do you want your purpose to be solely focused on your family, career, to the community or to the whole world? Creative thinking always has something to do with the way you come up with your purpose. You do not want to have a purpose only because it was suggested. Of course, you want something that only you can have and also think about the ways in which you will accomplish them.

The enthusiasm to be in complete trust of your quest should enable you to learn a number of life lessons which will eventually offer you the best rewards that life has to offer. Be sure to define your intent in the most creative way with the right skills at hand and this will ensure that you will be on the right track.

Chapter 3

Define Your Motivator

Just like your purpose, motivation has a lot to do with the way you achieve your goals. It is a fuel that accelerates you when you feel like giving up on achieving what you want. With a high enough level of creative thinking, it should be easy for you to identify the things that motivate. Know how to give applicable definitions to your motivators using this chapter.

Motivation – Your Fuel to Improving Creative Thinking

Knowing how to determine your motivators in life is a major factor that will help you live a more fulfilled and happier life. Indeed, people have aspirations, goals and dreams in life and achieving them can be a great source of happiness and fulfillment in living.

You might have goals to lose weight, plans to achieve success in your relationship or career or dreams to pursue an interest or passion. However, without proper motivation, all of these may stay as dreams, goals and plans, particularly when you're not motivated enough to achieve them and turn them into a reality.

Certainly, you would like to see your real worth in life and it can be attained by being able to perform things that you really like, things you are capable of, do something for others and make yourself and other people happy. When you seem to have an insufficient amount of motivation try some of the following tips to boost it back up.

❏ *Stay Positive*

Positive thoughts play a significant role in your life's outlook and in providing you with motivation to reach your goals. If you stay optimistic while thinking that you can accomplish a task assigned to you, or by thinking that you will be able to obtain your goals, you should feel motivated to take the necessary steps needed to achieve it.

❑ *Seek Inspiration From The People And Things Around You*

Whether it is great relationships from family and friends, or the beauty of nature, being able to seek out ideal inspiration always provides positive effects in making yourself feel motivated to finish things. Therefore, try to make great relationships and maintain a satisfactory rapport with your family.

❑ *Mind Your Health And Deal With Stress In Life Effectively*

Stressed and tired bodies will most likely result in motivation insufficiency, preventing you from doing your tasks. Perform exercises on a daily basis. This will not only make you physically stronger, but it will also improve your mood which will help you to effectively deal with different challenges in life every day.

❑ *Break Your Routine*

One of the many things which may contribute to motivation insufficiency is executing the same thing each day and being stuck in a routine without knowing your direction in life. Sometimes, it is good to explore new opportunities, discover other interests and develop new skills. Do not be afraid of taking risks, exploring new ways of obtaining your goals and getting out of your comfort zone sometimes to explore new things you find around and make the most out of new life opportunities.

❏ *Know The Purpose Of Everything You Do*

Most likely, you feel motivated when there is some sense of need to do something. Coming up with the purpose of why you are living your life every day will really make things easy, as it helps you maintain your motivation. Having your efforts dedicated to something you treasure and love can also turn out to be a good motivator. Whatever challenges you need to face in life, as long as you think of it as something you do for your loved ones, you will certainly find yourself feeling motivated and confident to do it.

With the right mind-set and creative thinking, you should find it easy to define your motivator. Once you execute all these pointers you can easily and quickly spot the things that give you motivation and be able to use them for further development of your skills. To find a motivator, you need not look too far. You should realize that searching for motivation in life may guide you in living a happier, more fulfilling and better life. Hence, make sure to do it for yourself.

Chapter 4

Make It a Challenge

"Every child is an artist. The problem is how to remain an artist once he grows up." – Pablo Picasso

Thinking creatively requires a wide and imaginative mind, which can accommodate all ideas possible. This is how creative thinking becomes a challenge and you can take advantage of this challenge to further extend the scope of your mind. Learn how to do the challenge by continuing with this chapter.

Make It a Challenge for Your Benefit

Have you ever thought about what it means to think creatively? As mentioned in the previous chapters, there is no single meaning to define creativity. However, creativity may be defined as the way to view things uniquely and a way to see various things. Being original, thinking "out of the box", finding a number of solutions to a certain problem and knowing how ideas are processed are few of the positive impacts of creative thinking.

If you want to overcome the challenges brought forth by creative thinking, the following hints should be very useful.

> *Thinking "Out of The Box"*

Thinking this way means you have to think differently. Do not just think of the usual things, but rather use you own creativity. Do not always go with what is usual. You can take a much more different path that only you can do. Thinking out of the box means you will have to alleviate yourself from thinking the common. Instead, go for those things that only creative people like you know exist and are possible. Also, take note that no new idea must be discarded just because it has never been considered before. Hence, by considering this challenge, you get to ask yourself to think unusual and differently.

> *Search For The Answers*

To perform this activity, you can come up with a number of questions that allow you to think. "What would happen if I open my mouth wide when I speak?", "When you think of the color blue, what emotions do you produce?", "What makes the wind blow?", "Why is looking directly at the sun bad for your eyes?", "What makes my pet happy?" To put it simple, let your imagination simply run wild!

> *Produce Some Psychological Distance*

Even though it has long been considered that refraining from a given task is helpful to break through the creative block, it may also seem that producing some "psychological" distance might also turn out to be useful. Based on a certain study, participants were able to resolve twice the number of impending issues when requested to consider the task's source as distant, instead of being close in proximity.

Try imagining your creative assignment as being distant and disconnected from your existing location or position.

According to the research, it might make a problem even more accessible, while encouraging a higher level of creative thinking.

Chapter 5

Arrange Your Surroundings

While using your creative thinking, you are not only using your brain to make it work. There are many other factors that allow a person to use their creativity and one of them includes the environment. Learn how surroundings affect the way a person thinks creatively by reading this chapter.

Your Surroundings Do the Trick

Try to complete a project or assignment in a messy or noisy room. Do you think you can accomplish it? Certainly, you can't. Maybe, you can finish the task, but not with the efficiency you can get from working in a conducive and clean environment. Indeed, the surroundings of the space where you are staying do play a very crucial role in letting you think creatively.

With the right choice of environment or by simply arranging your surroundings properly, there is a high chance for you to make the most of your creative thinking. Ever since the early times, human beings have needed to be sensitive with their environment in order to survive. This means that you have a natural awareness of your environment and you look after that environment with particular qualities.

The transition in your surroundings along with the laughter and chitchat in the background, the whirring of a coffee machine and the cups clattering will possibly set off your creative fuel in no time.

Know how to create the perfect environment towards creative thinking with the following ideas:

- *Sound*

People often think that when you concentrate on producing useful ideas, you must stay inside a quiet room. However, you need to realize that noise is not essentially bad. Actually, an average noise level of about 70-80 dB (decibel) points, may help in promoting your creative thinking.

- *Color*

Choosing the right color for your working environment may also play a crucial role. For instance, if you are going to pick between blue and red as your desktop background color, what would you choose? You can answer this by thinking about the things that normally enter your mind when you think of either the two. What comes to your mind when you see or talk about color blue? It can be the sky or the ocean.

What about red? The color red triggers people to think about red light, ambulances, emergencies, stop signs and blood. All of them are dangerous or mistake signs. This basically leads people to be in an avoidance mode and hence, become more vigilant and cautious. Accordingly, you do well on a detailed oriented task. However, when the main task is naturally more creative, blue is considered to be a better option. Still, depending on your preferences, you can find a color pattern that works for you.

- *Temperature*

You want to be comfortable while trying to be creative. It is advised that you find a temperature that makes you relaxed but also keeps you on point as well.

- *Lighting*

Try to think intuitively. In what light condition would you become more actively creative, in a bright room or in a dim one? People will usually choose the bright one over the other, yet you might actually find it quite the opposite.

What's the logic? It is the thing called "disinhibition". People basically control their behaviors. In the office environment, you always regulate your behavior, the way you sit, talk and more. If a room is finely lit, you might feel like each part of your body could be judged and observed by other people, allowing you to act accordingly. However, inside a dim room, your guard goes down a bit, allowing you not to have the need of controlling yourself rigorously. This is where your creative side enters the scene.

With a properly arranged surrounding, it becomes a lot easier for you to work with your creative thinking. So, make sure to consider all the pointers mentioned here.

Chapter 6

Set Aside Time

Time is required for everything, especially if it includes the goals that you want to achieve. So, if you want to produce and develop your creative thinking skills, you certainly have to set aside some time for it. Discover the best ways to incorporate your creative thinking practices into your routines as you read this chapter.

Giving Time Is Crucial

Creative thinking or daydreaming is very important and it can help you accomplish other essential goals. So, how do you do it? Check out the following ideas to learn more.

- *Take Time*

This does not necessarily mean that you need to spend almost half of your day just staring at the ceiling or messing with a stress ball. Remember that you still need to complete your tasks and excessive "creative thinking" can be a massive issue.

On the other hand, when you plan your day carefully, including some time for relaxation, while letting your mind drift, it can create a significant difference. It does not necessarily need to be a significant amount of time, such as one hour, but a couple of minutes throughout the day can do it.

Or, rather, try having a certain regular activity replaced with creative thinking. Rather than browsing through Facebook while drinking a morning coffee, you can sit at your office chair and look out of the window. You probably take a long break before getting back to work after lunch rather than surfing for worthless news, stroll around the building, making your mind clear.

- *Creating Thinking Is Not Wasting Time*

You are probably wondering about the difference between creative thinking and wasting time. In reality, it is a fine line. Maybe, not all stargazing may be useful. However, viewing the stars might result in a few real revelations within your life. The way you utilize this information will completely depend on you.

Finally, you are the one to decide whether or not you are being productive or you're just wasting your time.

Once you take a seat for your regular "creative thinking time", make sure to start cranking the ideas out. To think over the issues and problems with the company is surely fine, but do not think that you need to concentrate on them. Creative thinking can work for each of the business aspects and they may include areas that you would like to widen in the future.

All it takes is a simple idea that can bring you a large amount of potential. Therefore, make sure to consider your time-wasting minutes as one of your business tasks. Doing all things needed may be the origin of the results, but looking up at the stars for your dreams can be a way to turn them into reality.

Chapter 7

Cut Down Interruptions

In order to think creatively, you have to eliminate all the possible interruptions that can potentially affect your mind. When you are concentrated and strategizing on future projects, your attention will suddenly be disturbed if you are interrupted by someone. How do you avoid or cut interruptions down?

Interruptions Bring Your Mind into Chaos

You will surely feel irritated as you find that interruptions are eating up your concentration. They can be the people around you, an email, a phone call or maybe a text message. While facing this continuous hail of chaos, you will probably wonder how you will be able to get anything done. To cut down the interruptions, you may want to consider the following tips and be able to obtain the highest level of creative thinking possible.

- **Assign Dedicated Work Periods**

Sometimes, interruptions are simply not allowed. In fact, when possible, try to find a tranquil space where you can carry on with your work and be able to think creatively. Choose a place in which you won't be viewed as available. If it is impossible, you may produce a system through which you can warn others that you can't be disturbed, like an email auto-responder or placing a card saying "Do not disturb".

- **Create A Standardized Process**

There are particular forms of interruptions, which spring from ambiguity. To put it simple, when people are not certain of where to have their request submitted or who is the person working on the request, normally, they will bother you to figure it out. A simple way to resolve this issue is to form a standardized process, while ensuring that everyone knows it.

The standardized process must include a single central channel for all templates and requests that simply solve the problem of confusion. In this way, when you want to use your creative thinking to form a more useful and successful project, you will not be disturbed by those unrelated and unnecessary disturbances from people around you.

- **Clear Up Your Mind**

Before you get into the process of creative thinking, make sure that you have a clear mind, which will provide more space for your incoming ideas. It is important to have a clear mind and dedicate time to create the ideas you would like to produce. If you have a cluttered mind, it will be easy for you to get distracted, thinking about when you will pay your bills, submit your projects or talking to your wife because you had a fight can hinder creative thinking. Make sure to think about these things and more beforehand so as to make the process all-time successful.

By greatly cutting down those interruptions you will be on your way to making the most of your creative thinking skills and you will even be able to develop and improve them for the better. This should allow you to create more useful ideas in the future.

Chapter 8

Master Your Skills

Creative thinking skills are highly required, especially in this modern and competitive world. Without these skills, it becomes hard to survive in today's different situations. So, if you have these skills, make sure to maintain and master them, as they can give you great benefits in the long run.

Be an Expert Creative Thinker

Having the required creative thinking skills is far too beneficial. These are things that no one can take away from you, so keeping such skills must be a priority. One of the main bases to creative thinking is lateral thinking or association. There are basically four behaviors that feed it, namely networking, experimenting, observing and questioning.

With the use of these behaviors, it will be easy for you to master your creative thinking skills. Hence, how do you go about with each of them?

- *Questioning*

Creative thinkers basically ask questions in two different ways. Either they impose restrictions on the question's parameters, or they ask queries that eradicate restrictions.

To achieve this, question-storming is recommended. Determine the problem that you are trying to solve. However, rather than brainstorming the solutions, you only need to brainstorm queries to the issue. Until those are answered, you probably will not know the best way to form a truly fine solution. To finish, prioritize your top 3 to 5 questions which must be initially addressed. Furthermore, encourage others to imagine the future through asking "what if" questions.

- *Observing*

As a marketer, business owner or any other profession you might have, it is important to be more observant because you surely like to guarantee that you truly understand what others think you are doing. With the aim to improve your creative thinking skills, observing what other masters are doing may do the trick. You can observe what other new tricks and strategies are used by others in order to develop and maintain their skills. You do not just have to be a creative thinker, but you also need to be a keen and observant in the market.

- *Experiment*

Experimentation is another strategy considered by many creative thinkers. If you want to improve your skills, you surely need to try more innovative and newer ideas at hand. You can experiment through the use of different concepts you see in the modern market. While there are a lot of successful people who are creative thinkers, it should be easy for you to find your motivation or inspiration to work it out. Based on their collective experiences, you can then come up with your individually unique ideas towards the development of your creative thinking skills.

- *Networking*

One innovative method used by many business people and others as well, who wants to attain success, is networking. Admit it that you cannot do things on your own. In one way or another, you will look for the help of other people. This is where networking embraces you with open arms. You can certainly use this strategy to enhance your creative thinking skills. Through networking, you will be able to share your thoughts to other people and you can also benefit from them by using their unique ideas. This is a two way process that both parties can certainly gain benefits from.

It is recommended to use a more unique and diverse network to get a better opportunity to come up with a creative solution. If you are going to become more creative with problem solving, you have to obtain input from other people who can provide a varied perspective, especially from those who view things differently than you. If you can have dialogues regarding problems or challenges you are facing and obtain some new perspective, you are more likely to come up with some creative ideas.

Chapter 9

Why You Must Be Creative

Creativity can be a way to reach success. It is something that many people have in order to move forward towards their goals. Hence, having some of it is truly beneficial and important. But, why do you really need to become creative? Learn why with the following chapter.

Creativity Is Close To Success

Creative thinking surely becomes a necessary and important skill that every individual looking to reach success should possess. This skill falls under the highest level of cognitive development. To be able to think creatively, you are required to use the both sides of your brain, while initially understanding many factors of underlying knowledge. Creative thinking skills are very important for success and achievement in today's world. That is why parents and adults are promoting it to their children at their early stages.

Young children are truly excellent creative thinkers. They continuously use their imaginations for holding "conversations" using play phones and many other things they do to play. That is why it is better for them to develop these skills, even at an early age. This should reap them a good harvest in the long run.

The same holds true with today's adults. Everyone certainly needs some amount of creative thinking in order to continue with their goals, for

business people to thrive with their businesses; for teachers to teach their students effectively; for students to finish with their studies; for engineers to build innovative and excellent structures; for designers to design new ideas, and simply everyone else in between.

With creative thinking at hand, you surely have the fuel to drive yourself down the path of success!

9 789339 855628

Printed by Libri Plureos GmbH in Hamburg,
Germany